His Return, a Comedy. Opus 53

HIS RETURN

A COMEDY

Opus 53

HIS RETURN

The nicely furnished boudoir in Mrs. Hartley's home in a small Northwestern town. There are three doors. The central one leads into the hall; that on the right into the interior of the house; that on the left into a bathroom. There is the furniture one would expect; a dressing table, a chaise-longue, two or three dainty chairs, and a pier-glass at one side. On the dressing table are two large framed photographs.

At the rise of the curtain the stage is empty. There is a pause. Then there enters John Hartley, a man of thirty-five or forty, dressed in a Canadian uniform.

He is very much excited. He is returning home after an absence of years. He enters as if he expects to find his wife here. She is not. He is disappointed, but he takes visible pleasure in going about the room, identifying the many familiar objects which it contains. He stops abruptly at the sight of the two portraits on his wife's dressing table, one of him, one of her. He takes up her picture, deeply affected, and kisses it.

There is a pause. Then he hears steps coming, and straightens up expectantly.

The maid enters.

THE MAID (*looking at him in surprise*)

How — how did you get in here?

HARTLEY (*smiling*)

Why, I walked upstairs.

THE MAID

Yes, yes, I know that. But how did you get into the house? I didn't hear the bell ring.

HARTLEY

I opened the door. (*As she looks her surprise, he shows a latchkey*) With this.

THE MAID (*with sudden comprehension*)

O–oh! Then you — you're the master! (*Hartley nods and smiles*) You're Captain Hartley! I'm so glad to see you! Why, I've heard all about you, and your medals, and being wounded, for three years! (*Timidly*) Might I — might I shake hands with you, Captain?

HARTLEY

Why, of course!

[*He shakes hands.*

THE MAID (*rubbing her hand delightedly*)

I never thought that I'd shake hands with a real hero!

HARTLEY

Hero? Bosh! They're *all* heroes over there! I'm just unlucky — wounded — sent home.

THE MAID

Nevertheless, the town's mighty proud of you!

HARTLEY

Shucks! I don't care about the town! Tell me: how is *she*?

THE MAID

The missis?

[*He nods eagerly. The maid starts abruptly, aghast.*

HARTLEY (*frightened*)

What is it? What's wrong?

THE MAID

She doesn't expect you until five o'clock!

HARTLEY (*laughing*)

I took an earlier train.

THE MAID (*dismayed*)

But why did you do that?

HARTLEY

Why? Is it so difficult to understand?

THE MAID

It was wrong.

HARTLEY

Wrong?

THE MAID

Don't you see? She wants to be dressed: to look her nicest, to receive you.

HARTLEY (*laughing*)

Well, what of that?

THE MAID

She'd be simply heartbroken if she knew that you'd gotten here, and she wasn't ready! You see, it's — it's something very special.

HARTLEY (*beginning to understand*)

Oh, something very special?

[*The door downstairs is heard to close.*

THE MAID

Here she is now!

HARTLEY (*delighted*)

Oh!

THE MAID

You won't spoil her pleasure?

HARTLEY (*sincerely*)

God forbid! (*he goes to the right-hand door*) Remember — half an hour upstairs will seem almost as long as three years over there!

[*He goes out. The maid waits until she hears approaching footsteps. Then she, too, goes. There is a pause. Then Helen Hartley enters in a street dress.*

HELEN (*turning, and calling to a person following her*)
Come right in, Sylvia.

SYLVIA (*entering. She is a pretty, brainless, young girl*)
Mrs. Hartley —

HELEN (*correcting her*)
Helen.

SYLVIA
Helen dear, will you do me a favor?

HELEN (*smiling*)
Who's the man?

SYLVIA
Your husband.

HELEN
What?
[*She takes off her hat.*

SYLVIA
May I stay here — till he comes?

HELEN (*shaking her head gently*)
No, dear.

SYLVIA
I'm simply dying to meet him!

HELEN
Do you want me to tell you a secret? So am I! (*As Sylvia pouts*) I haven't seen him in three years.

SYLVIA
I've never seen him at all!

HELEN (*simply*)

I'm his wife. . . Child, child, when you've been married as long as I have, you will understand — if — *if* you and the lucky man who gets you love each other as dearly as — well, as *we* do!

[*She takes up Hartley's photograph.*

SYLVIA

Oh, but we will!

HELEN (*smiling, and petting her*)

That's right! Be happy! Be as happy as I have been! (*She pauses*) There are moments in life that are like no other moments. There was one in my life when he asked me a question, and I said yes; and there was another when we knelt together in church; and there was another, but that wasn't so pleasant, when I waved good-by to him from the station platform, when he joined the Canadians three years ago — (*she pauses*) and there will be a wonderful moment, a moment for which I have been living ever since, when he comes home to me. (*Kindly*) Don't you see? There mustn't be any third person here? Just he — and I!

SYLVIA (*contritely*)

I'm so sorry, Mrs. Hartley.

HELEN (*with an abrupt change of manner*)

Now, now! Don't call me Mrs. Hartley! It makes me feel so old! Ugh!

SYLVIA (*smiling, and kissing her*)

Helen, dear!

HELEN

And don't be so respectful! I don't like it when young girls are so respectful to me; treat me just as they would their mothers! I'm not old! I'm only thir — I'm only — (*She breaks off*) Well, it's nobody's business how old I am, is it?

SYLVIA

Of course not!

HELEN (*slowly*)

Not that there's any secret about it. . . . (*She smiles at Sylvia*) But what I wouldn't give to be your age again! (*Tapping Sylvia's cheek*) It didn't take paint to put *that* color on, did it?

SYLVIA (*embarrassed*)

Oh, Mrs. Hartley!

HELEN (*resignedly*)

There you go again: Mrs. Hartley! (*Sighing*) I suppose it's the right thing, anyhow, isn't it?

SYLVIA

You old darling! (*Helen winces at the word. Sylvia picks up her wraps*) You want me to go now, don't you?

HELEN (*looking at her shrewdly*)

Would you like to help me dress?

SYLVIA

Would I?

HELEN

Then I'll read you his last letter!

[*She rings for the maid.*

SYLVIA

From over there?

HELEN (*shaking her head*)

No; written the moment he landed here — to let me know when he'd arrive.

[*The maid enters.*

THE MAID

Yes, ma'am?

HELEN

Bring me the dress. You know which one?

THE MAID (*smiling*)

I know, Mrs. Hartley.

[*She goes to the clothes closet.*

HELEN (*turning to Sylvia*)

The same dress I wore the day I said good-by to him at the train!

SYLVIA

What a charming idea!

HELEN (*producing a letter*)

His letter suggested it. Listen: "My own dearest girl—" (*She reads to herself: looks up*) No, I can't read the beginning. (*She reads a little further silently*) No, I really can't. (*She goes ahead*) Ah! Here's something!

SYLVIA (*with eager anticipation*)

Yes?

HELEN (*reading*)

"The weather on the trip home was lovely."

SYLVIA

How intensely exciting!

HELEN

It's not very satisfactory, is it? (*By this time the maid has changed her shoes. She indicates them*) The same shoes I wore that day! (*She reverts to the letter*) Ah!

SYLVIA

Yes?

HELEN (*After an instant's hesitation*)

I'm going to read this to you. Some day *you* may get letters like it. (*She reads*) "Do you know what image has been in my mind every minute for the last three years? Do you know what picture was before my eyes as I lay in that shell hole, wounded, expecting every instant to be my last? It was your face, dear, as the train pulled out of the station, your face, dear, and your smile, your smile put on to encourage me, for God knows there was no smile in my heart — that day. Every detail is as distinct as if you stood before me as I write — the little dress you wore: it was always my favorite — (*she indicates the dress in the maid's hands*) — the hat: one of the kind that came down over the side of your face — (*she indicates it*) Do you remember how it was in the way when —*"

She drops her voice so that it is inaudible, and continues.

SYLVIA

What was that last, Helen?

HELEN

"Every detail; yes, every detail — "

SYLVIA

But the hat? What did he say about the hat?

HELEN

(*Rises. By this time the maid has unhooked her dress*) This is the hat. Don't you like it?

[*She thrusts it into Sylvia's hands, and changes quickly into the second dress.*

SYLVIA (*putting down the hat, and looking at the dress*)

Do you know, I used to have a dress something like

that? (*She watches the maid attempt to hook it up*)
That's not the way to do it! Mayn't I hook you
up, Helen?

HELEN

If you'd like to.

[*She nods to the maid, who goes out.*

SYLVIA (*taking the maid's place*)

I'll feel that I've had some share in preparing for him!

HELEN (*dreamily*)

His favorite dress!

SYLVIA (*working very hard: panting*)

Mrs. Hartley!

HELEN

Well?

SYLVIA

I believe — I believe — you've grown stout!

HELEN

What?

SYLVIA

I can't close more than half of the hooks!

HELEN (*horrified*)

I never thought of trying it on until to-day! (*She
hurries to the pier glass, followed by Sylvia. She looks:
then, in horror*) Oh-h!

SYLVIA (*laughing*)

What?

HELEN

Oh! Oh!

SYLVIA

Helen! Just because you've gotten stout?

HELEN

It's not that! Oh, no! It's not that! It's because

I've gotten old! Come here: stand beside me: look at yourself next to me! Do you see? . . . It's come! It's come! I always knew it *would* come — not gradually, so that I wouldn't know it, but all of a sudden, without a moment's notice — all at once! It was only three years ago that I said good-by to him, and I wore this dress. I was a young wife. To-day he's coming home to find me an old woman!

SYLVIA (*frightened*)

Why, Mrs. Hartley, that dress looks very becoming!

HELEN

It would — on you. Don't lie to me, please! I've lied to myself enough! I've painted and powdered and dined and danced with the youngest of them! But it had to come to an end. I knew it had to come to an end. But I hoped — *how* I hoped that it would not come to an end before to-day!

SYLVIA

Helen, dear — why — why —

HELEN

You can't say anything. There's nothing anybody can say. *I* used to say to myself that he'd find me as young, as beautiful, as the day I waved good-by to him at the station. Now — now I know that will never be. (*With horror*) He'll come home to find an old woman sitting opposite him at his own table! [*She weeps.*

SYLVIA (*nervously, after a pause*)

Helen dear, you can't be over —

HELEN (*interrupting*)

I can't be — but I am. They always *are* "over!" (*She pauses*) You know, it's not that I care what other people think: I don't give *that* for their opinions! He's the only one that counts. He used to love my youth; my freshness — and now, if he wants youth and freshness, he'll have to go somewheres else to get it! . . . (*She shakes her head bitterly*) Jealous? I have always hated jealous women! But to-day I understand: to-day I too am jealous, jealous!

SYLVIA

Mrs. Hartley!

HELEN (*coming to a hysterical calm*)

I don't mean you, child. Of course not! You'll pardon me, won't you? Just the excitement — the excitement of knowing that he was coming home. (*She has led the way to the door*) You'll go now, Sylvia?

SYLVIA

I'm so sorry, Mrs. Hartley!

[*She goes.*

HELEN (*closing the door after her*)

So sorry! So sorry!

[*She laughs bitterly; walks to the dressing table; takes up the letter: reads it over again with obviously tragic feelings.*

THE MAID (*entering*)

Ma'am!

HELEN (*wearily*)

Yes?

THE MAID

He's come!

HELEN (*taken aback*)

What?

THE MAID

He's just come in!

HELEN (*an instant of indecision. Her first impulse is to rush to the door*)

Tell him to wait!

THE MAID (*astonished*)

To wait?

HELEN

You heard what I said? And come back when you've told him.

[*The maid goes. Even before she has crossed the threshold, Helen has torn off the dress, and flung a wrap around her shoulders. She rushes to the table, sits down, and begins rubbing off her paint madly. The maid reenters.*

HELEN

Bring me my black and gold!

THE MAID (*astonished*)

Your black and gold?

HELEN

And quickly!

THE MAID

Yes, ma'am.

[*She hurries to the closet, and takes out a third gown.*

HELEN

Put me into it.

THE MAID

But I thought — but I thought —

HELEN (*hysterically*)

That I was going to wear the other one? How absurd! What on earth made you think that? (*The maid stares at her, simply dumfounded*) Never mind. I'm so excited that I don't quite know what I'm saying. You can wear the other dress, can't you?

THE MAID (*incredulously*)
The blue and white?

HELEN
Yes.

THE MAID
Yes'm. I can wear it.

HELEN
Then take it. It's yours.

THE MAID
Oh, thank you, ma'am.

HELEN
Now — I'm ready. Show him in.
[*The maid goes off with the dress. Immediately she is out of sight, Helen rushes off through the left-hand door. There is a pause. Then Hartley enters softly.*

HARTLEY
Helen! Helen dear! (*He advances into the room*) Where are you? Where are you, dear?
[*Helen reënters. She has finished removing every vestige of paint and powder from her face. She has suddenly become herself — a beautiful woman.*

HARTLEY
Helen! (*They rush into an embrace. Presently*) Isn't it wonderful to be home again?

HELEN
John!

HARTLEY
To walk the streets of my own town! To stand under the roof of my own house!

HELEN
Is that all, John?

HARTLEY (*shaking his head with a smile*)

No; that isn't all.

HELEN

Say it, John! Say it!

HARTLEY

To feel your arms around my neck! To feel your lips pressing mine! (*He kisses her*) Do you realize what I've been through for three years?

HELEN

We'll try to forget that.

HARTLEY

We'll try! (*He holds her off at arm's length*) And now!

HELEN

Now!

HARTLEY

Let me look at you!

HELEN (*in a strained voice, after a little pause*)

Well?

HARTLEY (*surprised at her tone*)

What is it?

HELEN (*excitedly*)

Tell me what I know already! Let me say it for you! That I've grown old, old, old! (*He tries to interrupt. She continues without a break*) You are not the only one who suffered these three years! I suffered! God knows how I suffered! For any reason — for no reason — when your letters didn't come — when the newspapers told of heavy fighting — when I stayed awake all night, worrying my soul out, I suffered, I suffered too!

HARTLEY

My dear!

HELEN

Let me finish! These wrinkles — do you see them? These lines — they were not here three years ago— do you know why I have them? They are for you, you, you! It's not the men alone who go through hell! It's the women they leave behind them!

HARTLEY (*taking her in his arms violently*)

My dear, dear girl! How I should love every wrinkle in your face — if there were any! Only there aren't!

HELEN

John!

HARTLEY

You old? That is what comes of looking too much in your mirror! A woman is only as old as she looks in the eyes of her lover!

HELEN (*almost gasping*)

And I?

HARTLEY

I have never seen you look so young, so beautiful, so altogether charming!

HELEN (*presently*)

John!

HARTLEY

Yes?

HELEN

Look what I've found!

HARTLEY

What?

HELEN (*with childish delight*)

A gray hair — in your moustache!

HARTLEY (*laughing*)

I've grown old, haven't I? (*As they separate an*

instant, a surprised look comes into his eyes)
Helen!

HELEN

What is it?

HARTLEY *(clapping his hands together)*

By Jove! What a fool I was not to see it!

HELEN

See what?

HARTLEY

And after the maid warned me that you had a surprise in store for me!

HELEN *(utterly bewildered)*

What is it, John?

HARTLEY *(triumphantly)*

You're wearing the same dress you wore the day you saw me off at the station!

[*She falls into his arms, laughing happily.*

THE CURTAIN FALLS

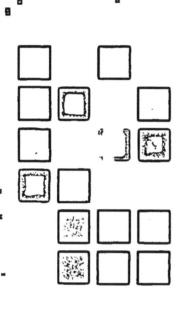

Lightning Source UK Ltd.
Milton Keynes UK
UKHW051019100920
369617UK00006BA/670